The Whitney Wolfe Herd Biography

Transforming the Dating Game and Building a Billion-Dollar Brand

Michael D. Maloy

All rights reserved. No part of this publication may be reproduced, distributed, or transmitted in any form or by any means, including photocopying, recording, or other electronic or mechanical methods, without the prior written permission of the publisher, except in the case of brief quotations embodied in critical reviews and certain other noncommercial uses permitted by copyright law.

Copyright © Michael D. Maloy, 2023

Table of Contents
Introduction
Chapter 1
Chapter 2
Chapter 3
Chapter 4
Chapter 5
Chapter 6
Chapter 7

Introduction

In the enormous canvas of modern relationships, the emergence of online dating has been a revolutionary force, transforming how individuals interact and find love. Amid the multiplicity of dating services, one name jumps out - Whitney Wolfe Herd. The tale of her life and successes matches the evolution of the dating game itself, reflecting the fusion of invention, empowerment, and business savvy.

Picture a world where love and connections are just a swipe away. It's a world that Whitney Wolfe Herd not only traversed but also greatly affected. The story begins in the digital domain, a space where algorithms connect hearts, and profiles encapsulate the spirit of those seeking love. Here, Whitney Wolfe Herd emerges not merely as a player but as a visionary who rewrote the laws of the game.

As we go into the biography of Whitney Wolfe Herd, it is crucial to realize her significant impact on the tech industry. From her early days at Tinder to the founding of Bumble, Wolfe Herd's path has been a testament to her ability to recognize gaps in the industry and pioneer novel solutions.

The tech business, previously dominated by male figures, discovered a powerful force in Wolfe Herd, challenging the established quo and offering a fresh viewpoint to the realm of digital connections.

Whitney's accomplishments extend beyond the limitations of dating apps. She had a crucial role in defining the narrative around female business in a male-centric industry. Her journey involves not just coding algorithms but breaking barriers, defying preconceptions, and motivating a generation of women to pursue their entrepreneurial goals in the tech sector.

At its core, this exploration strives to capture the incredible story of Whitney Wolfe Herd, a visionary entrepreneur who not only changed the dating environment but also developed a billion-dollar company. From her early experiences at Tinder to the launch of Bumble and beyond, Wolfe Herd's tale epitomizes the dynamic convergence of technology, commerce, and societal transformation.

The thesis depends on evaluating the multiple facets of Whitney's impact - from the creative features that transformed the user experience on dating apps to the broader ramifications of her work on gender dynamics and equality within the digital industry.

As we walk through the phases of her life, the objective is to uncover not only the business techniques that fuelled Bumble's success but also the attitude that separates Whitney Wolfe Herd as a pioneering character in the contemporary tech world. This research is not only a biography but a trip into the growing world of online connections and the lady who had a vital role in shaping its course.

Chapter 1

Background and Upbringing

Whitney Wolfe Herd's journey into the IT business and her eventual impact on the dating environment are firmly based on her formative years. Born on July 1, 1989, in Salt Lake City, Utah, Whitney's childhood laid the framework for her future endeavors. Her parents, Michael and Kelly Wolfe, instilled in her the principles of hard work, perseverance, and the significance of education.

Growing up in a close-knit household, Whitney demonstrated early signs of perseverance and ambition. Her passion for technology began to bloom throughout her adolescent years, a time when the digital world was quickly unfolding.

Observing the revolutionary impact of the internet, she acquired an intuitive fascination with its potential and the ways it may redefine communication and connections.

Despite enduring certain obstacles common to adolescence, Whitney's supportive familial environment gave her the basis to pursue her ambitions. Her early exposure to technology and the growing internet era inspired her interest in the possibilities that lay ahead.

Whitney Wolfe Herd's introduction into the tech business gathered momentum during her tenure at Southern Methodist University (SMU) in Dallas, Texas. Pursuing a degree in International Studies, she displayed a remarkable interest in both global issues and the fast-expanding digital scene. It was at SMU when Whitney's trajectory collided with the realm of mobile apps and web platforms.

In 2012, fresh out of college, Whitney joined the emerging startup Tinder, which was swiftly gaining traction as a groundbreaking dating software. Her involvement as a co-founder and the company's Vice President of Marketing marked the beginning of her substantial contributions to the dating software industry.

At Tinder, Whitney played a significant part in building the app's image and user experience, contributing to its quick rise as a cultural phenomenon.

Whitney's early experiences at Tinder were essential in forming her perspective of the online dating world. It was at this era that she realized both the promise and limitations of current platforms, setting the stage for her future business ventures. However, her stint at Tinder was not without its problems, eventually leading to a key choice that would alter the path of her career.

The Co-founding of Tinder and the Decision to Embark on a New Path

Tinder, launched in 2012 by Sean Rad, Jonathan Badeen, Justin Mateen, Joe Munoz, Dinesh Moorjani, and Whitney Wolfe Herd, swiftly became a cultural sensation. The app's unique swipe-right-to-like and swipe-left-to-pass functionality transformed the way consumers approached online dating. However, with the tremendous success, internal dynamics at Tinder proved increasingly problematic for Whitney.

In 2014, Whitney Wolfe Herd made the difficult choice to leave Tinder, a move driven by alleged incidents of sexual harassment and discrimination. This departure represented a turning point in her career, but it also prepared the door for her to embark on a new path—one that would redefine her role in the digital industry.

empowered, comfortable, and in control of their online dating experience.

The concept of women making the first move was not only a strategic alteration in the user interface but a fundamental reworking of power dynamics inside the dating realm. This strategy attempted to challenge prejudices, develop courteous interactions, and create a more equal space for online contacts.

As Whitney designed Bumble, her vision stretched beyond the bounds of romantic connections. She saw an opportunity to build a platform that fostered not just dating but also friendships and professional ties. The objective was to develop a holistic ecosystem that catered to the different social requirements of its users, promoting Bumble as more than just a dating app.

Founding Bumble with Andrey Andreev and the Development Phase

With a clear vision in mind, Whitney Wolfe Herd sought a partner who shared her passion for innovation and knew the intricacies of the computer sector. Enter Andrey Andreev, the Russian entrepreneur and founder of the dating app Badoo. The collaboration between Whitney and Andreev signaled the beginning of a partnership that will determine the future of Bumble.

Whitney and Andrey brought complementary expertise to the table. While Whitney brought her firsthand knowledge of the dating app environment and a vision for empowering women, Andrey contributed his expertise in building software ventures. Together, they embarked on the ambitious journey of developing Bumble.

The development phase was a significant stage where the intellectual vision of

Bumble began to materialize as a practical product.

The team worked on designing an intuitive and user-friendly interface that resonated with the app's distinctive approach to online interactions. The technology infrastructure needed to enable millions of users to form connections, whether in romance, friendship, or professional networking, was methodically crafted.

Beyond the technological components, the team worked on developing a culture that represented the ideals buried in Bumble's DNA. The commitment to inclusivity, respect, and empowerment became the guiding principles that defined both the internal dynamics of the company and the user experience of the app.

As the development phase continued, Whitney and Andreev encountered the hurdles inherent in introducing a product that attempted to upset existing standards. The team overcame technical hurdles, updated features based on user feedback, and fine-tuned the algorithms that powered Bumble's unique approach to pairing.

Launching Bumble and the Initial Reception

After months of development and anticipation, Bumble made its debut on the digital stage. The debut represented a critical moment not only for Whitney Wolfe Herd and Andrey Andreev but also for the millions of users seeking a fresh, empowering approach to online friendships.

Bumble's entry into the app world was received with a blend of curiosity, enthusiasm, and cynicism. The thought of women initiating discussions was a break from the usual, and the industry watched attentively to see how people would respond to this creative shift in dynamics.

The initial reception, however, exceeded expectations. Users welcomed the idea of Bumble as a platform that empowered women, and the app soon gained traction. The striking yellow branding, coupled with the attitude of placing control in the hands of women, set Bumble apart in a congested market.

The success of the launch was not just ascribed to the originality of the concept but also to the strategic alliances and marketing efforts deployed. Whitney Wolfe Herd's reputation as a vibrant entrepreneur and advocate for women in tech had a vital part in building interest and trust in the Bumble brand.

As users started to explore the app, Bumble's commitment to safety and courteous communication became clear. The platform introduced features to enhance user experience, including photo verification and the incorporation of user preferences to tailor matches. These features contributed to developing a positive and secure atmosphere for consumers to navigate the online dating market.

The initial reception set the scene for Bumble's rapid expansion. The app's unique approach resonated not only with women but with users across the gender spectrum who applauded the shift towards more courteous and egalitarian online interactions. Bumble became more than a dating app; it became a symbol of a societal shift in how people viewed connections in the digital age.

The debut of Bumble demonstrated the successful execution of Whitney Wolfe Herd's concept. The software was not only a technological innovation but a social experiment testing established beliefs about gender roles in online interactions. As Bumble gathered momentum, it became obvious that the convergence of technology and empowerment might change not only the dating game but the entire landscape of social interactions.

Chapter 3

Entrepreneurial Challenges

Whitney Wolfe Herd's entrepreneurial journey is distinguished by perseverance and determination, but it also involves substantial hurdles that challenged her mettle as a corporate leader. One of the most crucial moments in her career occurred when she decided to leave Tinder, the dating service she co-founded.

Leaving Tinder was not a decision taken lightly. In 2014, Whitney severed ways with the organization amidst a backdrop of internal upheaval. The departure, however, was not without its challenges. It signaled the beginning of a judicial struggle that would bring to light concerns of sexual harassment and discrimination.

Wolfe Herd filed a complaint against Tinder, alleging not only discrimination but also sexual harassment by her co-founder and then-boyfriend, Justin Mateen. The case shined a spotlight on the poisonous culture within the firm and the obstacles encountered by women in the male-dominated tech industry.

The court fights that proceeded were emotionally and professionally draining for Whitney Wolfe Herd. They were not only about pursuing justice for herself but also about tackling bigger concerns of workplace culture and gender dynamics in the IT world. The action finally settled out of court and became a chapter in Whitney's life that underlined the hurdles faced by women in their quest for achievement and equality in the workplace.

Overcoming Setbacks: From Discrimination Allegations to Building Resilience

The aftermath of the legal battles with Tinder cast a shadow, but Whitney Wolfe Herd emerged from the experience with a reinvigorated sense of purpose. The setbacks and obstacles she endured became the crucible for establishing resilience, both emotionally and professionally.

The discrimination charges brought to light the stark reality of gender bias in the computer business. For Wolfe Herd, however, this served as a spark for change. Instead of succumbing to the hurdles, she utilized them as fuel to propel her resolve to create a more inclusive and empowering environment for women, not just within the workplace but also in the products she envisioned.

The experience of resolving discrimination claims marked a critical turning point in

Whitney's entrepreneurial trajectory. It fuelled her resolve to develop a startup that not only rocked the dating app industry but also challenged traditional gender conventions. The wounds of the court battles became a source of strength, defining Whitney's determination to promote a culture of equality and respect in her future activities.

Building resilience in the face of hardship required not only personal strength but also a strategic approach to her profession. Whitney Wolfe Herd transformed her experiences into advocacy, becoming a strong voice for women in computing. She used her platform to speak out against gender discrimination and to encourage programs that fostered diversity and inclusion within the industry.

Bumble's Early Struggles and the Commitment to a Unique Vision

The launch of Bumble signified a fresh start for Whitney Wolfe Herd, but it was not without its early problems. The software business is fraught with rivalry, and creating a new dating app involves overcoming existing companies and convincing customers to embrace a creative approach.

Bumble's distinctive selling proposition—the empowerment of women in initiating conversations—was both its strength and its potential challenge.

In the early days of Bumble, there were naysayers who questioned the sustainability of a dating app where women made the first move. Breaking away from established standards always involves a risk, and Bumble's success rested on convincing users that this shift in dynamics was not simply a gimmick but a fundamental enhancement in the online dating experience.

The dedication to a unique vision needs strategic planning and good communication. Bumble's marketing efforts underscored not just the app's functionality but also its ethics. The startup positioned itself as more than a dating platform; it was a movement questioning traditional standards and cultivating empowerment. Whitney Wolfe Herd's commitment to this goal permeated every part of Bumble's branding and user experience.

In the early years, Bumble faced the issue of attaining critical mass. Convincing people to accept a new platform in a congested market needed novel techniques. The team at Bumble had to traverse the difficulties of user acquisition, ensuring that the app's distinguishing features were not merely enticing on paper but converted into real interactions for its users.

The dedication to a unique vision also meant risking potential opposition. As

Bumble gained notoriety, it became a target for individuals reluctant to change or uncomfortable with upsetting traditional gender roles. The app endured criticism and examination, emerging stronger with each setback.

The early problems of Bumble, from convincing consumers to embracing a fresh approach to withstanding industry resistance, were fundamental to its evolution. These hurdles, rather than deterring Whitney Wolfe Herd, formed the building pieces for Bumble's success. The commitment to a unique vision not only set Bumble apart but also established the framework for its disruptive impact on the dating landscape.

Whitney Wolfe Herd's journey from leaving Tinder amidst legal disputes to overcoming hurdles and establishing Bumble as a unique force in the dating app business is a monument to her perseverance and steadfast commitment to her goal. The struggles she endured not only formed her as an entrepreneur but also provided the framework for Bumble's rise as a cultural and technological disruptor in the realm of online interactions.

Chapter 4

The Bumble Revolution

Bumble's groundbreaking approach to online dating, where women take the initiative by making the first move, has altered the mechanics of digital connections. The influence of this concept goes beyond mere utility; it has become a symbol of empowerment, challenging traditional gender norms and encouraging a more courteous and equal online atmosphere.

1. Empowering Women in Online Interactions

The underlying premise of Bumble—the empowerment of women—reshapes the power dynamics common in traditional dating applications. By allowing women to initiate discussions, Bumble not only offers them agency but also alters the narrative from a passive role to an active one.

This empowerment extends beyond the app, impacting cultural attitudes toward women's responsibilities in dating and relationships.

2. Reshaping Online Conversations

The "women make the first move" idea has important consequences for the nature of online communication. By placing control in the hands of women, Bumble fosters an environment where encounters begin on a basis of mutual interest and permission. This adjustment lowers unsolicited messages and helps to a more positive and courteous user experience.

3. Cultural Impact and Symbolism

The significance of this concept goes into the cultural world, where Bumble has become a symbol of a bigger movement fighting for gender equality. Whitney Wolfe Herd's mission to empower women through the platform has resonated with people who seek a more progressive and inclusive approach to online networking. The "Bumble woman" is not merely a user; she embodies a philosophy of agency and autonomy.

Bumble's Expansion Beyond Dating into Friendships and Professional Connections

Bumble's vision transcends the confines of traditional dating applications. Recognizing the varied nature of human connections, Whitney Wolfe Herd pushed Bumble's expansion into realms beyond romance, establishing a comprehensive social platform that promotes not only dating but also friendships and professional networking.

1. Bumble BFF: Redefining Friendships in the Digital Age

Understanding that meaningful interactions extend beyond romantic relationships,

Bumble created BFF mode. This tool allows users to locate like-minded persons for platonic friendships. By using the same "women make the first move" approach, Bumble BFF facilitates connections based on shared interests, hobbies, and values, creating a space for users to broaden their social networks.

2. Bumble Bizz: Networking in the Digital Professional Landscape

Bumble's dedication to offering a full social experience extends to the professional realm with Bumble Bizz. This tool fosters networking and career contacts, allowing users to broaden their professional circles. The popular concept of women initiating conversations transfers into the professional realm, upsetting established networking practices.

3. Creating a Social Ecosystem

The development of friendships and professional relationships transforms

Bumble into a social ecosystem. Users can smoothly switch between modes, seeking love relationships, friends, or business contacts inside the same site. This adaptability portrays Bumble as more than a dating app; it's a one-stop-shop for varied social demands, reflecting the complexity and diversity of human connections.

Navigating Controversies and Maintaining Brand Integrity

In the dynamic landscape of the tech business, addressing disputes is an inherent component of a company's path. For Bumble, keeping brand integrity throughout adversity has been a strategic objective. From court challenges to public criticism, Whitney Wolfe Herd and her team have proven tenacity and a commitment to the ideals that define the Bumble brand.

1. Addressing Controversies Head-On

Bumble has encountered its share of issues, including legal disputes and complaints about its approach to gender dynamics. However, the corporation under the direction of Whitney Wolfe Herd has been proactive in tackling these difficulties. Open communication, transparency, and a dedication to continual development have been crucial aspects in handling conflicts while staying true to the brand's beliefs.

2. Cultural and Social Impact

As Bumble's profile has risen, so too has its cultural and societal impact. The platform's stance on issues such as gender equality, online safety, and inclusivity has positioned it as a thought leader in the internet sector. Bumble's support for establishing a positive and courteous online community has contributed to shaping industry discourse and influencing user expectations.

3. Brand Evolution and Adaptation

Maintaining brand integrity involves a fine balance between being true to basic values and reacting to the growing needs of users and the cultural landscape. Bumble has shown a readiness to evolve while remaining rooted in its core beliefs. The brand's evolution demonstrates a knowledge of the dynamic nature of the digital sphere and the need to be relevant in a quickly changing environment.

4. Community Engagement and User Feedback

Bumble's commitment to brand integrity is shown in its involvement with the user community. Actively soliciting and responding to customer feedback, addressing problems, and adopting changes based on user experiences have been crucial to sustaining a positive brand image. This two-way connection generates a sense of community and trust, key components in sustaining brand integrity.

The Bumble revolution involves not only the new approach to online dating but also the broader impact on cultural norms and expectations.

The empowering of women, expansion into friendships and professional relationships, and the skillful handling of controversies emphasize Bumble's remarkable trajectory. Whitney Wolfe Herd's idea has not only rocked the dating app business but also set a precedent for a more inclusive and courteous approach to online connections in the digital age.

Chapter 5

The Business of Bumble

The result of years of strategic growth and innovation, Bumble's decision to go public in 2021 represented a critical milestone in the company's path. The Initial Public Offering (IPO) was not just a financial milestone; it marked the confirmation of Bumble's unique approach to online interactions and the beginning of a new chapter in the business.

1. Strategic Timing and Market Conditions

Bumble's decision to go public was carefully calibrated, taking into consideration both internal variables and the broader market environment. The year 2021 featured a great climate for tech IPOs, with investor enthusiasm for creative and disruptive enterprises. Bumble utilized this momentum, matching its IPO with a period of heightened interest in the tech industry.

2. Financial Implications and Capital Infusion

The IPO was a mechanism for Bumble to raise funds, driving additional expansion, technology breakthroughs, and potential acquisitions. The infusion of capital through the public offering gave Bumble the financial strength to execute strategic goals and solidify its position in the competitive online dating and social networking scene.

3. Public Perception and Brand Visibility

Going public not only had financial effects but also altered public perception and brand visibility. Bumble's IPO attracted extensive media coverage, shining a spotlight on the company's achievements and its unique approach to online interactions. The public offering upgraded Bumble's position from a privately held unicorn to a publicly traded firm, gaining visibility among investors and users alike.

Achieving Unicorn Status and Whitney Wolfe Herd's Status as a Self-Made Billionaire

The journey from a startup to earning unicorn status—an industry designation for privately owned companies valued at over $1 billion—was a tribute to Bumble's quick growth and market relevance. Whitney Wolfe Herd's status as a self-made billionaire further underlined the success not only of the company but also of her entrepreneurial vision and leadership.

1. Unicorn Status: A Symbol of Success

Bumble's climb to unicorn status positioned the company within an elite group of high-valued startups. This position was reached through a variety of variables, including user growth, revenue generation, and investor confidence. Bumble's ability to disrupt established dating app models and grow into more social categories helped to its valuation, making it a symbol of success in the tech industry.

2. Whitney Wolfe Herd: Architect of Success

The journey to unicorn status and beyond was inextricably related to Whitney Wolfe Herd's leadership. As the architect of Bumble's success, she led the company through hurdles, grasped opportunities, and steered the ship toward strategic expansion. Whitney's role as not simply a CEO but also a visionary leader played a significant element in establishing Bumble's future.

3. Self-Made Billionaire: A Personal Triumph

Whitney Wolfe Herd's status as a self-made billionaire was not only a financial milestone; it signified a personal achievement against the backdrop of hurdles experienced by women in the software industry. Her trajectory from co-founding Tinder, and enduring legal challenges, to launching Bumble as a billion-dollar company displayed strength, inventiveness, and a commitment to uplifting women in digital environments.

Analyzing the Highs and Lows of Bumble's Stock Performance

Following the euphoria of going public, Bumble's stock performance became a focus point for investors, analysts, and the broader market. The highs and lows of Bumble's stock journey reflected not only the company's financial performance but also the dynamic nature of the tech sector and the online dating business.

1. Post-IPO Surge and Initial Enthusiasm

Bumble's stock experienced a spectacular launch, witnessing an immediate rise in value post-IPO. The market's enthusiasm for the new approach to online relationships, coupled with optimism about Bumble's growth potential, contributed to the favorable trajectory. Investors were lured to the company's unique position in the market and its ability to expand beyond traditional dating.

2. Challenges and Market Volatility

Despite the initial enthusiasm, Bumble, like many startup businesses, suffered problems and market instability. Factors such as macroeconomic conditions, industry trends, and competitive dynamics influenced the stock's performance. Bumble's experience reflected the broader realities of the stock market, where volatility is not commonplace, especially for newly public companies.

3. Analyst Assessments and Earnings Reports

Analysts played a vital part in analyzing Bumble's stock performance, making assessments based on financial indicators, industry trends, and the company's strategic activities. Earnings reports became key milestones, revealing insights into user growth, revenue generation, and the efficiency of Bumble's development into new social categories.

4. Long-Term Vision and Investor Confidence

Amidst the highs and lows, Bumble's long-term vision and strategic objectives had a vital part in molding investor confidence. The company's ability to adapt to market changes, develop in response to user needs, and maintain a commitment to its basic values reinforced the perception of Bumble as a viable long-term investment.

5. Impact of External Factors

External factors, such as adjustments in user behavior, changes in the competitive landscape, and global events, have an influence on Bumble's stock performance. The COVID-19 pandemic, for example, affected online dating habits, impacting user interest and revenue streams. Navigating these external challenges became a part of Bumble's continuing difficulty in maintaining a resilient stock performance.

The company of Bumble incorporates not just financial achievements such as going public and obtaining unicorn status but also the personal victories of its founder, Whitney Wolfe Herd. Analyzing the highs and lows of Bumble's stock performance provides a detailed knowledge of the dynamic nature of the tech industry and the company's resiliency in the face of market setbacks.

The journey from IPO to stock performance shows not just financial indicators but also the evolving story of a company that has revolutionized online connections in the digital age.

Chapter 6

Leadership Transition

The news of Whitney Wolfe Herd's intention to stand down as CEO of Bumble was a pivotal point in the company's existence. After over a decade in the leadership of the dating app giant, Wolfe Herd's choice to transfer into the role of Executive Chair generated both curiosity and suspicion among the tech world.

1. Founder's Reflection and New Horizons

Whitney Wolfe Herd's decision to stand down as CEO was not a sudden or rash move. It indicated a founder's reflection and a desire to explore new frontiers while keeping a strategic role inside the organization. In her views on the decision, Wolfe Herd hinted at a new and exciting job that would allow her to return to her founder origins, bringing passion and focus to the next phase of Bumble's growth.

2. Maturation of a Visionary Leader

Wolfe Herd's stint as CEO saw the evolution of Bumble from a dating app into a multi-faceted social platform. The maturity of her leadership style and strategic vision played a vital influence in Bumble's evolution. As she stepped back from the day-to-day operations, it was not only a personal evolution but also a testimonial to the durable structures and leadership team she had established over her tenure.

3. Continued Influence and Executive Chair Role

Despite stepping down from the CEO position, Whitney Wolfe Herd's choice to assume the job of Executive Chair reflected her continuous dedication to Bumble's success. The Executive Chair post allowed her to continue active in high-level strategic decisions, leveraging her experience and ideas while potentially exploring new possibilities for the company.

Introduction of Lidiane Jones as the New CEO

The advent of Lidiane Jones as the new CEO of Bumble offered a fresh perspective to the company's leadership. Jones, a seasoned digital executive with experience at firms like Salesforce and Slack, comes into the post with a mandate to shepherd Bumble through its next chapter of development and innovation.

1. Jones's Background and Tech Expertise

Lidiane Jones's hiring as CEO of Bumble was not arbitrary. With a background in technology and managerial roles at notable firms, Jones brings a plethora of knowledge to the table. Her stint at Salesforce, particularly in digital experiences, highlighted her awareness of the growing tech landscape—a key skill for a company like Bumble managing the convergence of technology and human connections.

2. Leadership Style and Cultural Fit
The installation of a new CEO invariably generates questions about leadership style and cultural fit. Jones's leadership style, steeped in her experience at tech titans, foreshadowed a potential shift in how Bumble will tackle obstacles and possibilities. The cultural fit between Jones and Bumble's principles would play a critical role in retaining the company's identity while stimulating innovation under new leadership.

3. Strategic Vision and Future Initiatives
As the new CEO, Lidiane Jones was tasked with creating Bumble's strategic vision and driving the firm into its next chapter of growth. Her experience in digital experiences and technology suggested a

potential focus on boosting user engagement, and technological breakthroughs, and maybe exploring new possibilities for Bumble's expansion beyond its existing services.

The Implications for Bumble's Future and the Industry

The leadership turnover at Bumble has consequences not only for the firm itself but also for the broader online dating and social networking industry. The decisions made by Wolfe Herd and the strategic direction outlined by Jones would influence how Bumble positioned itself in a competitive market and address increasing user expectations.

1. Continuity and Innovation

The transition represented a careful balance between continuity and innovation. While Bumble aimed to sustain the excellent trend set by Wolfe Herd, the new leadership presented a chance for fresh insights and initiatives. The problem came in ensuring that the key ideals that distinguished Bumble's success were retained while embracing innovation to stay ahead in a changing business.

2. Market Perception and Investor Confidence

The market's assessment of the leadership shift played a role in shaping investor confidence. How investors reacted to the news, the response to Jones's strategic vision, and the company's ability to communicate a consistent narrative about its future orientation all contributed to molding market opinion. Bumble's stock performance in the wake of the shift would be extensively studied as an indicator of investor confidence.

3. Competitive Landscape and Industry Trends

Bumble's leadership transition occurred within the context of a rapidly expanding online dating and social networking landscape. The sector was undergoing developments in user behavior, technical advancements, and responses to societal changes. The decisions made by the new leadership would situate Bumble within this changing landscape, defining how well it could react to evolving trends and keep its competitive edge.

4. User Experience and Innovation in Online Connections

The user experience on Bumble was essential to its success. The leadership move sparked doubts about how the company would continue to emphasize and enhance the user experience. Innovations in functionality, user interface, and responsiveness to user feedback would be key in ensuring that Bumble remained a favored platform for individuals seeking online interactions.

5. Social Impact and Advocacy
Bumble, under Whitney Wolfe Herd's leadership, had positioned itself as a platform with a social impact goal. The transition brought forward doubts about how the corporation will continue to push for causes such as gender equality, internet safety, and diversity. Bumble's role as a thought leader in the industry would be influenced by its continued commitment to social impact activities.

6. Potential Expansion and Diversification
The leadership transition gave me an opportunity for Bumble to investigate possible development and diversification. Whether the company would launch new features, pursue partnerships, or enter new markets depended on the strategic vision articulated by Lidiane Jones. The decisions

made in this regard would not only determine Bumble's future but also influence the broader landscape of internet interactions.

The leadership transfer at Bumble showed a complex balance between continuity and change. Whitney Wolfe Herd's decision to step down as CEO and Lidiane Jones's introduction brought forth a set of considerations that expanded beyond the company's internal dynamics to affect the industry at large.

As Bumble managed this transformation, the consequences for its future were entwined with how it positioned itself in a quickly expanding digital landscape and responded to the demands of users, investors, and societal developments.

Chapter 7

Legacy and Impact

Whitney Wolfe Herd's path as a female entrepreneur has not only made an indelible effect on the IT business but has also become a source of inspiration for aspiring women in the entrepreneurial scene. Examining her contribution entails going into the hurdles she faced, the milestones she reached, and the broader impact on the story of female entrepreneurship.

1. Navigating a Male-Dominated Tech Landscape
Whitney Wolfe Herd's early years in the software industry were distinguished by the obstacles of navigating a mostly male-dominated landscape.

The male-centric culture, frequently characterized by gender bias and discrimination, provided difficulties for women trying to establish themselves as leaders. Wolfe Herd's experiences at Tinder, including her exit amidst legal disputes, emphasized the fundamental faults underlying the sector.

2. Founding Bumble: A Response to Gender Dynamics

The founding of Bumble was not merely a business initiative; it was a conscious response to the gender dynamics prevalent in the online dating sphere. Wolfe Herd's choice to build a platform where women had the agency to make the first step defied traditional power systems.

Bumble became a symbol of empowerment, allowing women a forum where they could assert themselves in a previously male-driven narrative.

3. Advocacy for Inclusion and Equality

Wolfe Herd's commitment to female business extends beyond Bumble's success. She emerged as a prominent advocate for inclusion, diversity, and gender equality in the IT industry. Her advocacy extended beyond words; Bumble's corporate culture echoed these ideals, creating an environment that supported diversity in leadership and championed programs targeted at bridging the gender gap in IT.

4. Mentorship and Support for Women Entrepreneurs

Wolfe Herd's career as a trailblazer included a commitment to mentorship and support for women entrepreneurs. Recognizing the value of mentorship in managing the hurdles particular to women in business, she became a guiding force for emerging female executives. Initiatives and activities under her guidance geared at fostering the next generation of women entrepreneurs displayed a commitment to establishing a more inclusive business landscape.

5. Impact on Female Funding and Investment

The significance of Whitney Wolfe Herd's contribution to female entrepreneurship extended to the area of fundraising and investing. As a successful female founder, her presence in the sector challenged established preconceptions about the types of ventures that could survive. Bumble's success in going public further emphasized the viability of firms founded by women, impacting investment patterns and creating a more egalitarian approach to fundraising.

6. Championing Work-Life Balance and Flexibility

Wolfe Herd's leadership style at Bumble also spurred talks surrounding work-life balance and flexibility. By creating policies that promoted a healthy work environment, including flexible working arrangements and an emphasis on employee well-being, she proved that successful entrepreneurship did not have to come at the cost of personal fulfillment and balance.

7. Cultural Shifts in Entrepreneurial Narratives

Examining Whitney Wolfe Herd's contribution to female entrepreneurship reveals broader cultural developments in entrepreneurial narratives. Her accomplishment defied perceptions and brought up conversations about the prospects for women in traditionally male-dominated sectors. The cultural influence goes beyond individual achievements, impacting how society perceives and values the role of women in determining the future of business.

The Cultural Impact of Bumble on Modern Dating

Bumble's introduction into the online dating scene represented a cultural revolution in how individuals perceive relationships, interactions, and the mechanics of modern dating. Analyzing the cultural impact requires evaluating the specific features introduced by Bumble, the response from users, and the broader implications for societal norms surrounding dating.

1. Women Making the First Move: Redefining Dating Dynamics

The core characteristic of Bumble—women making the first move—had major ramifications for dating dynamics. In a landscape historically defined by men taking the lead, Bumble's approach defied gender conventions and encouraged a more equal and respectful way to begin contact. The cultural impact expanded beyond the site, influencing talks about agency and equality in dating.

2. Fostering Respectful and Inclusive Conversations

Bumble's emphasis on courteous communication became a cultural touchstone. By allowing women to manage the initiation of interactions, the platform hoped to reduce instances of unsolicited messages and promote a more courteous online dating atmosphere. The impact was visible in user testimonials and discussions across the site, with users embracing the shift towards more meaningful relationships.

3. Expanding Beyond Traditional Dating Norms

Bumble's cultural impact goes beyond typical dating boundaries. The creation of Bumble BFF and Bumble Bizz showed a realization of the varied nature of human connections. The platform's adaptability in allowing not just sexual relationships but also friendships and professional connections contributed to a broader cultural discourse about the altering nature of social interactions.

4. Influence on Competitors and Industry Trends

The success of Bumble influenced competitors and industry trends in the online dating arena. The app's unique features, along with its cultural messaging, forced other platforms to reassess their tactics. Conversations around permission, polite communication, and diversity gained prominence, impacting how the industry as a whole responded to consumer expectations.

5. Impact on Gender Dynamics and Equality

Bumble's cultural effect overlapped with issues about gender dynamics and equality in partnerships. The platform presented a real example of how technology may be exploited to disrupt established power dynamics. By enabling a space where women felt empowered to take the lead, Bumble contributed to broader talks about equality in both online and offline relationships.

6. Challenges to Stereotypes and Stigmas

Bumble's cultural impact extends to addressing prejudices and stigmas linked with online dating. The platform positioned itself as a forum for thoughtful and respectful encounters, opposing myths that characterized online dating as solely casual or shallow. Bumble's popularity helped to change opinions about the legitimacy and possibilities for meaningful relationships through digital platforms.

7. Influence on Offline Dating Behavior

The cultural effect of Bumble extended the digital arena, impacting offline dating behavior. The platform's emphasis on respect, agency, and purposeful connections inspired users to approach dating with a more thoughtful perspective. The influence on how individuals managed not just online encounters but also real-world dating circumstances demonstrated the rippling effects of Bumble's cultural messaging.

Whitney Wolfe Herd's Role as a Trailblazer for Women in Tech

Whitney Wolfe Herd's influence as a trailblazer for women in the computer business extends beyond her accomplishments as an entrepreneur. It incorporates her advocacy for gender equality, her commitment to fostering inclusive workplaces, and the larger impact of her leadership on changing preconceptions about the role of women in technology.

1. Breaking Barriers in the Tech Industry

Wolfe Herd's foray into the tech business and subsequent success broke established barriers and prejudices. The male-dominated nature of the industry had long been a disincentive for women, but Wolfe Herd's journey proved that not only could women succeed in computing, but they could also lead and invent in ways that altered entire sectors.

2. Advocacy for Inclusion and Diversity

As a trailblazer, Wolfe Herd became a prominent champion for inclusion and diversity within the computer industry. Her leadership at Bumble was defined by a commitment to building a culture that mirrored these ideals. Initiatives promoting diversity in recruiting, mentorship programs, and an emphasis on fostering a culture of inclusion demonstrated a proactive approach to eliminating gender barriers.

3. Inspiring the Next Generation of Women in Tech

Wolfe Herd's accomplishment served as encouragement for the next generation of women joining the tech profession. Her journey from co-creating Tinder to founding and leading Bumble became a tale that contradicted the notion of a glass ceiling. By sharing her experiences and views, Wolfe Herd actively contributed to encouraging other women to pursue professions in technology and business.

4. Cultural Impact Beyond Bumble

While Wolfe Herd's role as a trailblazer was prominently connected with Bumble, her impact stretched beyond the bounds of the organization. As a visible and accomplished woman in computing, her presence influenced industry discourse and led to a broader societal shift. Wolfe Herd became a symbol of the evolving narrative around women's roles in technology, challenging conventional preconceptions, and inspiring change.

5. Intersection of Feminism and Tech Innovation

Wolfe Herd's status as a trailblazer also emphasized the confluence of feminism and tech innovation. Her devotion to empowering women through Bumble's platform and her advocacy for gender equality within the firm positioned her as a leader who understood the transformative potential of technology in furthering feminist values.

6. Balancing Leadership and Advocacy

Wolfe Herd's groundbreaking journey included a difficult balance between leadership responsibilities and advocacy activities. While bringing Bumble to success, she simultaneously used her platform to support topics connected to women in IT. This dual function emphasized the varied nature of modern leadership, where success was not only judged by financial measures but also by the positive impact on societal narratives.

7. Navigating Challenges and Resilience
As a trailblazer, Wolfe Herd faced hurdles peculiar to women in leadership roles. From legal battles to industry scrutiny, she displayed resilience in the face of hardship. Her ability to persist and lead with conviction created a precedent for women handling comparable hurdles in the tech sector.

Assessing Whitney Wolfe Herd's legacy and influence entails comprehending her numerous contributions to female entrepreneurship, the cultural impact of Bumble on modern dating, and her role as a trailblazer for women in tech. Through her journey, Wolfe Herd not only revolutionized the landscape of internet relationships but also became a symbol of empowerment and change in an industry that continues to battle with issues of diversity and equality.

Her legacy reaches beyond business data, affecting the narrative of what is achievable for women in technology and entrepreneurship.

CONCLUSION

Whitney Wolfe Herd's revolutionary path stands as a tribute to the power of resilience, inventiveness, and a creative approach to entrepreneurship. From her early career at Tinder to co-founding Bumble and molding it into a billion-dollar company, Wolfe Herd's story is one of overcoming hurdles, fighting for change, and reshaping the dynamics of the online dating market.

1. From Tinder to Bumble: Navigating Challenges and Seizing Opportunities

Wolfe Herd's adventure began at Tinder, where she co-founded the platform and played a vital part in its early success. However, her resignation amid legal disputes signaled a turning point.

Instead of surrendering to hardship, Wolfe Herd saw an opportunity to address the gender issues common in the online dating sector. The conceptualization of Bumble, with its unique feature of letting women make the first move, highlighted her ability to transform obstacles into inventive solutions.

2. Entrepreneurial Resilience: Overcoming Setbacks and Legal Battles

The legal issues surrounding Wolfe Herd's exit from Tinder should have been a barrier for many, but she approached them with bravery and purpose. The cases not only highlighted structural concerns within the IT industry but also became fuel for Wolfe Herd's commitment to building a platform that championed women's agency and empowerment.

The capacity to overcome setbacks and turn adversity into an opportunity is a hallmark of her entrepreneurial path.

3. Building a Cultural Movement: Bumble Beyond Dating

Wolfe Herd's goal for Bumble extends beyond the realm of typical dating applications. The platform's expansion into Bumble BFF and Bumble Bizz demonstrates a dedication to establishing meaningful connections in all spheres of life.

The cultural movement sparked by Bumble moved beyond sexual connections, influencing friendships, professional networking, and societal conversations regarding gender dynamics.

4. Advocacy for Equality and Inclusion: A Personal and Corporate Commitment

One of the defining elements of Wolfe Herd's path is her continuous commitment to campaigning for equality and inclusivity. From developing a working culture at Bumble that promotes diversity to leveraging the platform as a vehicle for social impact, Wolfe Herd's efforts have surpassed the confines of business.

Her advocacy became not simply a part of Bumble's corporate ethos but also a personal quest to combat prejudices and pave the way for a more inclusive future.

5. From CEO to Executive Chair: A Strategic Evolution

The recent change from CEO to Executive Chair represented a significant evolution in Wolfe Herd's role inside Bumble. It marked a purposeful decision to pull back from day-to-day operations and embrace a new and exciting period of growth.

The move demonstrated Wolfe Herd's ability to adapt, delegate, and exploit her skills in directing the firm from a strategic angle, underscoring her dedication to the future development of Bumble.

The Ongoing Legacy of Bumble and Its Founder

As Whitney Wolfe Herd turns into the role of Executive Chair, the continued legacy of Bumble shows not just the success of a dating app but a cultural movement that has altered the way individuals approach relationships and connections. The impact of Bumble extends beyond the digital arena, impacting society norms, changing gender relations, and leaving an indelible stamp on the landscape of online interactions.

1. Bumble's Continued Innovation: A Pioneer in the Industry
Bumble's legacy is marked by its continuing commitment to innovation. The platform's ability to provide features that transcend traditional dating norms—empowering women, encouraging friendships, and promoting professional connections—demonstrates a continual focus on satisfying the shifting requirements of users.

As Bumble continues at the forefront of the online dating business, its legacy is entwined with a commitment to staying ahead of the curve.

2. Impact on Competitors and Industry Trends

Bumble's success has influenced competitors and industry trends in the online dating arena. The cultural influence of features such as women making the first move and the emphasis on courteous chats pushed other platforms to reassess their tactics. Bumble's effect is obvious in the industry's growing focus on user agency, safety, and meaningful relationships, altering the trajectory of online dating experiences.

3. Championing Social Impact: Beyond Profit to Purpose

Bumble's legacy extends beyond financial achievement to its commitment to social impact. The platform has actively engaged in programs addressing topics such as gender equality, internet safety, and inclusivity. Bumble's support for social issues and its position as a thought leader in pushing for good change contribute to a legacy that transcends profit margins and connects with a greater sense of purpose.

4. Corporate Culture and Inclusivity: A Model for the Industry

The legacy of Bumble is inextricably related to its corporate culture, established by the values supported by Whitney Wolfe Herd. The emphasis on inclusivity, diversity, and establishing a workplace that recognizes people as individuals has established a standard for the industry. Bumble's corporate culture serves as a model for other organizations aiming to develop settings that reflect the different opinions of their user base.

Final Thoughts on the Evolution of the Dating Industry and the Entrepreneurial Spirit of Whitney Wolfe Herd

Reflecting on the growth of the dating market and the entrepreneurial spirit of

Whitney Wolfe Herd uncovers a tale of transformation, empowerment, and the potential for technology to reshape societal norms. As the dating business continues to grow and as Wolfe Herd's story takes on new dimensions, it invites final reflections on the lasting legacy of both Bumble and its founder.

1. Evolution of the Dating Industry: From Stigma to Empowerment

The dating business has experienced a remarkable change, changing from a stigmatized sector to one that encourages individuals to take charge of their relationships. Bumble's contribution to this transformation goes beyond providing a platform for connections; it has contributed to shifting ideas about the possibilities and opportunities that online dating may bring.

2. Technology as a Catalyst for Social Change

Wolfe Herd's business career emphasizes the transformative power of technology as a catalyst for social change. Bumble's revolutionary features not only upset traditional dating relationships but also generated questions about consent, agency, and equality. The convergence of technology and society standards, as represented by Bumble, emphasizes the potential for digital platforms to be vehicles of constructive change.

3. Entrepreneurial Spirit and Impact Beyond Profits

The entrepreneurial ethos of Whitney Wolfe Herd is distinguished by a commitment to influence beyond profitability. Her trajectory reflects a broader understanding of entrepreneurship—one that embraces social responsibility, inclusivity, and advocacy for significant change. Bumble's success is not just evaluated in financial terms but in the enduring impression it leaves on societal narratives and the potential it opens for future generations of entrepreneurs.

4. Trailblazing Leadership: Shaping the Future of Tech

Wolfe Herd's status as a trailblazer goes beyond her particular accomplishment; it signals a shift in the narrative around women in technology. Her story acts as an example for women navigating the tech landscape and challenges conventional views about who can lead and innovate in the business. Wolfe Herd's trailblazing leadership has the ability to change the future of innovation by establishing settings that value diversity and inclusivity.

5. Legacy of Empowerment: Beyond Bumble's Walls

The legacy of Whitney Wolfe Herd and Bumble is one of empowerment that transcends beyond the digital confines of the site. It is a heritage that empowers women to take charge of their narratives, challenge conventional standards, and push for a more inclusive and respectful approach to relationships. The impact of this legacy is felt not only in the success of Bumble but in the broader societal conversations it has ignited.

In conclusion, thinking about Whitney Wolfe Herd's transformative path, the ongoing legacy of Bumble, and the evolution of the dating business brings to light a tale of innovation, empowerment, and societal impact.

As technology continues to impact the way we interact and as entrepreneurial leaders like Wolfe Herd create new paths, the convergence of business and societal change becomes a roadmap for a future where technology is not simply a tool for connections but a force for positive development.

Whitney Wolfe Herd's path is not just a narrative of entrepreneurial success; it is a story of rewriting the rules, changing standards, and creating an enduring legacy in the ever-evolving landscape of technology and human interactions.

Printed in Great Britain
by Amazon